MW00902237

# A Pioneer Farm Girl:

## *The Diary of Sarah Gillespie 1877-1878*

Edited by Suzanne L. Bunkers
with Ann Hodgson,
foreword by Suzanne L. Bunkers

Content Consultant:
Judy Temple, Associate Professor of Women's Studies and
English at the University of Arizona; editor of *A Secret to Be
Burried: The Diary and Life of Emily Hawley Gillespie 1858-1888*

## Blue Earth Books

an imprint of Capstone Press
Mankato, Minnesota

Blue Earth Books are published by Capstone Press
151 Good Counsel Drive, P.O. Box 669, Mankato, Minnesota 56002
http://www.capstone-press.com

Copyright © 2000 by Capstone Press. All rights reserved.
No part of this book may be reproduced without written permission from the
publisher. The publisher takes no responsibility for the use of any of the materials
or methods described in this book, nor for the products thereof.
Printed in the United States of America.

*Library of Congress Cataloging-in-Publication Data*
Gillespie, Sarah (Sarah L.)
A pioneer farm girl : the diary of Sarah Gillespie, 1877-1878 / edited by
Suzanne L. Bunkers with Ann Hodgson; foreword by Suzanne L. Bunkers.
p. cm. — (Diaries, letters, and memoirs)
Includes bibliographical references (p. 31) and index.
Summary: Excerpts from the diary of Sarah Gillespie, a pioneer in Iowa in the
nineteenth century. Includes sidebars, activities, and a timeline related to the era.
ISBN 0-7368-0347-5
1. Gillespie, Sarah (Sarah L.) Diaries Juvenile literature. 2. Girls—Iowa—
Manchester Region Diaries Juvenile literature. 3. Manchester Region (Iowa) Biography
Juvenile literature. 4. Manchester Region (Iowa)—Social life and customs Juvenile
literature. 5. Farm life—Iowa—Manchester Region Juvenile literature.
[1. Gillespie, Sarah (Sarah L.) 2. Frontier and pioneer life—Iowa. 3. Diaries. 4. Women
Biography.] I. Bunkers, Suzanne L. II. Hodgson, Ann. III. Title. IV. Series.
F629.M28G55  200
977.7'385—dc21                                                    99-29043
                                                                        CIP

**Editorial credits**

Editor: Chuck Miller
Designer: Heather Kindseth
Photo researcher: Heidi Schoof
Artistic effects: Louise Sturm-McLaughlin

**Photo credits**

State Historical Society of Iowa, 6, 7, 8,
11, 13, 14, 15, 17, 18, 20, 24-25, 27;
Gregg Andersen, 9, 22, 26

1 2 3 4 5 6  05 04 03 02 01 00

# CONTENTS

# *Editor's Note*

The Diaries, Letters, and Memoirs series introduces real young people from different time periods in American history. Whenever possible, the diary entries in this book appear word for word as they were written in the young person's original diary. Because the diary appears in its original form, you will notice some misspellings and mistakes in grammar. To clarify the writer's meaning, corrections or explanations within a set of brackets sometimes follow the misspellings and mistakes.

This book contains only portions of Sarah Gillespie's diary. Text sometimes has been removed from the individual diary entries. In these cases, you will notice three dots in a row, which are called ellipses. Ellipses show that words or sentences are missing from a text. You can find a more complete version of Sarah's diary in the book *All Will Yet Be Well: The Diary of Sarah Gillespie Huftalen, 1873-1952*. More information about this book is listed in the To Learn More section on page 31.

# FOREWORD

I started writing in a diary when I was 10 years old. At first, I wrote short entries about the weather, family activities, schoolwork, and friendships. I soon began to write about my thoughts and feelings. My hopes and dreams for the future eventually found their way into my diary. I have kept a diary for more than 35 years. Writing in it is still one of my favorite things to do.

Diaries like Sarah Gillespie's and mine are called primary sources. Primary sources are letters, photographs, diaries, and other materials that give firsthand accounts of people's lives. They detail the events and feelings people have experienced. We learn about personal views of history from primary sources.

Today, primary sources such as Sarah Gillespie's diary show us how people lived in the past. We learn about the challenges people have faced. We learn about their accomplishments. Their stories help us understand how past events have led to the present.

Suzanne L. Bunkers,
Professor of English and
Director of Honors Program,
Minnesota State University, Mankato

## *Sarah Gillespie:*
# A PIONEER FARM GIRL

Sarah Gillespie was born in Manchester, Iowa, on July 7, 1865. Sarah's parents, Emily and James Gillespie, were pioneer farmers who worked hard to make a living. Their 100-acre (50-hectare) farm in Iowa was near the edge of the United States' western frontier.

Pioneer farm families like the Gillespies led difficult lives. Many families had moved west to escape the overcrowded conditions of the eastern United States. Some of these families had never farmed before, and almost all of them were not used to the very different climate of the plains. Harsh winters, rainy springs, and dry summers made planting and harvesting crops difficult.

Pioneer farm families depended on one another to survive in this new environment. Experienced pioneers helped newcomers build their houses and raise their barns. At harvest time, pioneer farmers worked together to bring in their crops. Pioneers also helped each other on a daily basis. Families who had extra food would share with their less fortunate neighbors. It was not uncommon for a family who butchered a cow to send some of the best steaks to their neighbor's house.

Pioneers on and near the edge of the frontier often became lonely. The closest farm family probably lived more than a mile (1.6 kilometers) away. But pioneers made special efforts to visit one another. Neighbors kept one another from becoming discouraged.

*Sarah Gillespie and her brother, Henry, began doing chores on the family farm when they were young children.*

*Pioneer farmers helped one another harvest their crops. They threshed the harvested wheat by beating it to separate the grain from the plant.*

Farming was not a very profitable business. Few pioneer farm families were able to save any money after they had paid their taxes and their bills. Lacking money, pioneers had to find new ways to obtain farm tools, as well as food that they could not produce on the farm. Many pioneer families used the barter system. Pioneers traded extra crops or livestock to the local country store for the necessary items.

Pioneers often did not have livestock or crops to spare. They had to borrow supplies from a country store on credit or apply for a loan from a local bank. Many stores would not lend supplies on credit because pioneers took a long time to pay for them. And many banks made pioneer farmers use their farms as collateral for a loan. If the farmers could not pay the bank, the bank took their farm away.

Children also had to help out if a pioneer farm was to survive. Sarah helped her mother feed livestock, pull weeds in the garden, sew new clothes, cook meals, and clean the house. Sarah's older brother, Henry, helped their father raise crops, care for the livestock, and repair farm equipment.

In addition to performing their daily chores, many pioneer farm children attended school. Sarah and Henry walked to a one-room schoolhouse that was one-half mile (.8 kilometers) away from their home.

In her diary, Sarah wrote about her life as a pioneer farm girl in Iowa. She told about all the experiences and hardships her family faced. By reading selections from her diary, we can learn what life was like for many ordinary farm families during pioneer times.

# The Diary of Sarah Gillespie, 1877-1878

*January 1, 1877 –*

New years. I commence to keep a journal to day.
Sarah L. Gillespie . . .

*January 3 –*

It was so cold we could not go to school. making a
whip stalk.

Henry, Pa, and I took some hay down to Uncle
Jerome's and saw the new bridge. It is a very nice one and rests
on bars of iron. I got a spool of black thread for me. Henry got the
papers. Ma worked on her Sofa cushion. Warmer.

*January 16 –*

I helped all day so she could finish Pa's pants to go to "The Old Settlers Society"
to-morrow. I washed all of the dishes, got supper & dinner & made a first-rate
jonnie cake. Cold & Snow.

*In 1910, this photo was taken of the Gillespie family farmhouse near
Manchester, Iowa.*

# Make Johnnycakes

Johnnycakes, or journey cakes, were a popular food for pioneers. Johnnycakes provided pioneers with energy on long journeys. Johnnycakes also did not spoil quickly and were easily stored in saddlebags.  Ask an adult to help you with this recipe.

**What You Need**

2 eggs

1 cup water

3/4 cup milk

2 tablespoons vegetable oil

1 teaspoon salt

2 cups yellow or white
   cornmeal

vegetable oil for greasing

medium-sized bowl

large spoon

skillet

spatula

butter

maple syrup

**What you do**

1. Stir the eggs, water, milk, oil, salt, and cornmeal together in the bowl until smooth.
2. Heat the skillet. Pour 1 tablespoon of vegetable oil into the skillet.
3. Pour 1/4 cup of the batter into the skillet. Cook until the johnnycake is brown on one side. Turn the johnnycake over with the spatula to cook the other side. Repeat until all batter is used.
4. Serve the johnnycakes warm with butter and maple syrup.

   Makes 8 to 10 johnnycakes.

*A successful harvest was an important event for any pioneer farm family. Farmers could use their crops to barter for supplies at local stores.*

*January 22 –*

We are not going to School any more it is so lonesome up there with only 4 or 5 scholars. Ma worked, she has got a very sore toe, we are going to study at home the rest of the winter. ma says as soon as we get through this arithmetic she will get us another one. Pleasant but Cold.

*February 14 –*

To day is St. Valentines day. I did not send any Valentines nor did not get any. To day was the last day of our school. there were a good many there . . . Ma did not go.

*April 3 –*

I done 24 examples [arithmetic problems] to day. Henry done 19, we go to town, it is very muddy. Sunday evening Barrs livery Stable, the Agricultural Depot & the Blacksmith shop was burned. they saved all of the horses but none of the carriages, he [Dr. Barr] says that his loss is about $3000.00. Dr. Barr feels pretty bad over it, all that was left was a buggy-wheel & cook stove & they were all burnt, the stove was cracked & broken, too, it is to bad . . . Mud, Mud, Mud.

*April 17 –*

go to school we had 12 scholars, the boys act real mean. the teacher said that there was not 1 boy in the whole school that tended to his own business. Warm.

*July 7–*

To day I am 12 years old. Warm.

*July 28 –*

Went up to Uncles get some butter stay to supper. I have been sick with the belly-ache. all day yesterday & $\frac{2}{3}$ of to day & feel some better . . . Very warm.

# One-room Schoolhouses

Sarah Gillespie spent much of her childhood studying in a one-room schoolhouse. Many children in rural communities attended one-room schoolhouses in the 1800s and early 1900s. Students from farm families often attended school only during the summer and winter months. They had to help with chores on the farm during the spring planting and the fall harvest.

Most one-room schoolhouses were small and plain. They had low ceilings and hard benches on which students sat. A teacher's desk and a blackboard for writing out lessons stood at the front of the room.

A one-room schoolhouse had one teacher who was responsible for teaching younger and older students at the same time. The teacher divided students into groups by their age. The teacher then gave each age group an assignment to work on and moved around from group to group to teach them.

Teachers taught reading, writing, math, geography, and history every day. Some teachers also taught art and music once or twice a week. Children sometimes used chalk to do their individual lessons on black pieces of slate. These slate boards were expensive and could break easily if dropped. Not every school could afford slate boards.

Teachers sometimes punished children who misbehaved by slapping their hands with a ruler or hitting them on the hand with a thin tree branch called a switch. Parents often encouraged this type of punishment in the 1800s and early 1900s. Teachers also made students skip recess or

perform chores if they misbehaved. Children might be made to cut firewood for the woodpile or sweep the schoolhouse's floor if they misbehaved.

The teacher assigned chores to students even if they were not being punished. Older children hauled wood into the school and started a fire in the fireplace during cold weather. Younger students took turns hauling a bucket of water to the schoolhouse each day.

*August 6 –*

 Help ma & pa pull weeds in the strawberry patch. I just touched a little young Bird in the nest & all the rest jumped out. I am so sorry. If it would do any good I'd cry. Cool.

*September 18 –*

 Go to school. Ma has been married 15 years to day. We have a surprise party here this evening there were 23 in all. they [ma and pa] were married over again. we had supper all kinds of cake pie & best of all water mellons & musk mellons. they presented ma & pa with a set of glass dishes a real nice time we had. moonlight evenings now. Warmer.

*September 27 –*

we all go to the fair. we had a good time. I got 2 premiums 1 on cake & 1 on bread. Ma has the first premium on a great many things but a few in town are trying to make a fuss about it & say they are not worthy of a premium. ma is a little spunky about it. Foggy.

*Sarah's parents, James and Emily Gillespie , made sure their children had fun. Emily and James took Sarah and Henry to picnics and to state and county fairs.*

# Going to the Fair

Fairs were a time for pioneers to enjoy themselves and take a break from work. Farmers brought samples of their livestock, crops, and farm equipment to the fair. They entered their goods in competitions with other farmers. Judges awarded premiums to the best entries in each category. Premiums were prizes such as ribbons or money.

Besides winning prizes, fair competitions gave people the chance to share information. Farmers learned how to raise better cattle and grow different crops. Farmers also sold some of their products and learned about new farming methods.

Women and children had their own competitions. They entered homemade items such as cakes, breads, canned goods, needlework, and clothing to be judged for premiums.

*December 25 –*

got a motto on CardBoard & a pair of slippers, but the slippers were too small, ma is going to exchange them. Henry got a purse pair of clippers & perforated motto. Ma got pa a book "The Royal Path of Life," & ma got herself a morocco pair worth 2.00. they were very nice & a perforated board motto. We [Sarah and Henry] got a small Christmas tree (A limb of our plum tree) & we hung the presents on it, it looked quite nice. so we did not hang up our stockings. work on my Motto. "What is a home without a mother?" foggy, Rainy.

# Make Your Own Motto

Mottoes were popular in the 1800s. These short sayings usually expressed positive thoughts. Sarah's motto read "What is a home without a mother?" Women and girls sewed mottoes or painted them on paper. Sunday school teachers often used mottoes from the Bible to teach their classes. You can make a cardboard motto.

## What You Need

Flat piece of cardboard,
  8 inches by 10 inches
  (20 centimeters by
  25 centimeters)

newspaper
hole punch
ribbon
paints or magic markers

## What You Do

1. Cover a flat surface with newspaper. Place the cardboard on the newspaper.
2. Find a motto to display. You can write your own motto or find one that is already written.
3. Write or paint your motto on one side of the cardboard. You can draw pictures or other decorations around the motto. If you use paints, allow them to dry.
4. Punch a hole in each of the top corners of the cardboard.
5. Thread one end of the ribbon through the first hole and make a knot. Make sure the knot is on the side of the cardboard that does not have the motto.
6. Thread the other end of the ribbon through the other hole, and make another knot.
7. Hang the motto where you can see it every day.

*Sarah sometimes worked arithmetic problems in
her diary. At that time, paper was expensive and
had to be used wisely.*

*December 31 –*

> To day we bid good bye to our old year & wish that our journal will be filled
> with pleasant & bright hopes . . . Colder.

*March 17, 1878 –*

> I am perfectly ashamed of my journal there are so many blob & goose tracks
> (or as pa calls them hens tracks) all the way through. I must write better.
>
> > Last night the moon had a golden ring
> > To-night no moon we see.

*April 11 –*

> do not feel very well. make syrup. ma & pa went to town leave [Henry] & I at
> home. a beggar stop & a tin smith. I got awful lonesome. ma get some licorice.
> ma's 40 years old. Windy.

*April 18 –*

got our lessons. Pa go to town, get a letter from Mrs. Wood wanting me to learn a piece to speak next Sunday. Easter we are to have kind of Exhibition get some herring, hog Cholera Medicine, the papers, and a 10 cent piece changed into pennies for ma get caught in a rain storm . . . I took off my hat & then my Apron & covered up so as to keep dry, just as I got home it began to just pour down & then hail . . . If I had not run about ¾ of the way I would have got soaked through & through . . . Rain.

*May 3 –*

get lessons. our nice little colty died. pa cried. Betsy [the Gillespies' horse] felt very bad. we are all so sorry. Warm

Forgot to say all our little goslings were taken this morning very sudden. pa said they were just going down to the slough & all of a sudden the old goose flew up in the cow yard & made a great fuss. pa looked out of the stable but didn't think much about it, until we looked & looked & looked again, but could not find them. too bad. Henry & I went up to Morses to see their little wolves . . . Warm.

*May 22 –*

did not get lessons. help pa build a fence. We all go to aunt Hatties & see their nice baby & to uncles. while we were gone 13 of our nicest little turkeys smothered to death. ma felt so sorry about it. ma put an extra quilt over them & fastened with a stick. something she had never done before. Cloudy.

*Many pioneer farm women raised geese and ducks for food and to sell.*

# Predicting the Weather
# with the Old Farmer's Almanac

Sarah ends almost every diary entry with a comment about the weather. Pioneer farm families often tried to predict the weather. They could then determine the best time to plant and harvest crops. A useful tool for predicting the weather was the Old Farmer's Almanac. Robert B. Thomas founded this magazine in 1792.

Thomas invented a complex formula based on natural weather cycles to predict the weather in the United States. Using this secret formula, the almanac has correctly predicted the weather 80 percent of the time since 1792.

The almanac is published yearly and is the oldest continuously published magazine in North America. In addition to weather predictions, the almanac offers information useful to almost anyone. The Old Farmer's Almanac includes tide tables for those who live near the ocean, sunrise tables and planting charts for those who live on a farm, and recipes for people who like to cook.

*Pioneer farm women were responsible for household chores such as washing laundry and ironing.*

*June 3 –*

I am so sorry. those poor old Robins sit on the fence & cry for their little ones, which we think were killed in the hard rain. ma said in the night she thought she heard her turkeys but it must have been those poor little robins. I climbed the tree & ever one was gone. I think it is too bad, did not get lessons. Rain.

*June 10 –*

I forgot to say that 1 of our little ducks got lost some where & we could not find it. I think that it either got stung & it ran in under some of the shrubbery, or has got on its back & cannot get up. We are so sorry. That was yesterday. I mean (on sunday). it is too bad. help ma & etc. Get lessons. Cold.

*June 22 –*

get part of lessons. help ma. I am tired ma is ironing & I cannot write very good. Henry go fishing. Quite warm. I forgot to say that pa fell out of the Carriage & hurt his head.

*July 7 –*

I am 13 years old to day. go to Sabbath school wear my
new Pink Chambree dress. in the evening we all take a
ride . . . this is the way I have celebrated my 13th
birthday. Very warm.

*July 31 –*

To day is the last day of July. I help ma . . . just as we got
the turkeys & ducks in under some boards & in a box it
began to hail & rain.

I tell you it rained so hard that we could hear it over
two miles [3 kilometers]. pa said if it was a tornado that
we must go down cellar. it is blowing real hard &
raining now. Rain.

*August 8 –*

go blackberrying. A wolf caught one of the little lambs
but he had to let go of it & pa caught & carried the
little lamb down here. he was sure that it would die
but we (ma & [Henry] & I) got him & put some tar
on every place that it was bitten . . . the worst places
were very near the throat & on the eyelid. we tried
to feed it some milk. When the sheep came in the
yard we carried it out & it found its mother &
tried to eat but he acted as if it hurt him & he
is so very weak too by losing so much blood. but
I guess that he will get well. I hope so anyhow.
go to town and [get] a chance to ride both
ways. Warm.

# Preserving Fruits and Vegetables

During the 1800s, fresh fruits and vegetables were not readily available year-round. Pioneer farm families often preserved fruit in large amounts of sugar. They preserved vegetables in salt or vinegar. The fruits and vegetables did not taste good when preserved using these methods.

In 1858, John L. Mason introduced a new way to preserve fruits, vegetables, and jellies. Mason invented a glass jar with a sealing lid that was inexpensive and easy to use. Families prepared fruits and vegetables and placed them in these glass jars. They then sealed the lids onto the glass jars. Because no air was able to enter the jars, fruits and vegetables stayed fresh for a long time. Many pioneer farm families then were able to enjoy fruits and vegetables year-round.

*September 4 –*

Henry is 15 years old to day & Ma make a jelly cake & a common cake & put candles on.

the motto was this: "When first I saw your face so fair; my heart was filled with anxious care." I think it was very good.

*September 24 –*

[Ma] help me make a necklace to take to the fair. a flea has got onto me & I am just covered in blotches & they itch so I cannot hardly stand it. A wolf came right down to the slough & caught a sheep & I saw the wolf jerk the sheep until he got it down & then we hollowed & made just all the noise we could & he left it but he stopped every 2 or 3 rods & look around as if he were very much disappointed. Henry go a fishing. I help pa sort out sheep & lambs to take to fair . . .

*September 27 –*

We all go to fair have a good time. I took 2 mottoes. straw-work Lampnet & handkerchief. get the 2nd premium on my handkerchief & on my straw-work. my Lampnet & all my things but the mottoes were the only ones there I think I had right to have the 1st premium on them all. ma got quite a no. of Red & blue Cards. we entered Betsy in the wrong class or else we would have got the Red Card = $6.00. we entered her as a horse of all work & it ought to have been draft-horse's because she is so slow. Pleasant.

*October 5 –*

A wolf caught another lamb he caught it in the left side & tore the skin off in a very large place as large as Pas hand . . . The butcher would not buy so they [Sarah's mother and father] brought it back . . .

Ma put the skin that was torn down back in place & sewed the wool together then she sewed 2 thicknesses of cloth over it and sewed it to the wool . . . I hope it will get well.

Henry took the sheep up above the railroad & watched them for 2 hour's . . . I done the morning work . . . The Wolf came right down east of the house. Help ma. Warm.

# LIVESTOCK

Pioneer farm families owned a variety of farm animals. Some of these animals helped with the farm work. Farm families raised other animals for food. Cattle were a valuable source of beef and veal. Cow's milk was used to make butter, cream, and cheese. Pigs provided pioneer farm families with bacon, ham, and lard.

Pioneer farmers used horses and mules in the fields to pull carts and plows. A mule is the result of mating a male donkey with a female horse. Like a horse, a mule has a large body and strong muscles.

Oxen are cattle specially trained to work in the fields. Oxen are much stronger than horses or mules. They pulled plows and carts. When oxen became too old to work, farmers fattened and butchered them to provide beef for the family.

Sheep served many purposes on pioneer farms. Families clipped the wool from sheep and spun it into yarn to make clothing. Farmers also butchered sheep for their meat, called mutton. The sheep trimmed grass by grazing and fertilized fields with their manure.

Chickens were another source of food. Female chickens, or hens, laid eggs. Families butchered hens when they became too old to produce eggs. Male chickens, or roosters, served as natural alarm clocks. They would crow each morning in the early dawn hours.

Many pioneer farm families considered geese, turkeys, and other poultry a delicacy. They often ate poultry on important holidays or special occasions.

*October 27 –*

we all go up to Aunt Hatties, she cried because she was so glad that we came. I believe that she & John will separate. he wants to go to Nevada & she will not go & if he goes she says she will never live with him again . . . Chilly.

*November 28 –*

. . . we had part of a baked pig for thanks-giving dinner . . . it was a very beautiful day just like summer. Beautiful.

*December 25 –*

Christmas. Go up to Uncles . . .we had a good time. I got a Cocoanut, China candle-stick, wax candle (red), A yard of satin Ribbon & some crackers. Santa Claus was very good this time. Henry got the same. Cool.

*December 31 –*

to day is the last day of the year. go to town get 10 cents worth of paper & 10 cents worth of envelopes & 3 cents worth of candy & a 10 ct salt cellar.

I gave Henry and [Ma] each 6 sheets of foolscap & 6 envelopes for New Years, & Divided the candy equal. Get a ride both ways. Warmer.
good bye old year
I am ready for the new.
Amen.
I hope I will have as pleasant a time in 1879 as I had in 1878.

# Starting Your Own Diary

Sarah kept a diary to record details about her life. She wrote about her home, school, family, and activities. Her diary tells us about life in the 1850s. Sarah did not know people would read her diary. She wrote it for herself. But later she shared her diary so other people would know what life was like for a pioneer farm girl.

You can keep a diary to record the details of your own life. You can write about the weather, family activities, school, and friendships. Diaries are a place where you can write openly about what you think and feel. You are writing it for yourself. Diaries can become personal histories. Someday your diary might be a book like Sarah's.

## What You Need

*Paper:* Use a blank book, a diary with a lock, or a notebook. Choose your favorite.

*Pen:* Choose a special pen or use different pens. You might want to use different colors to match your different moods.

*Private time:* Some people write before they fall asleep. Others write when they wake up. Be sure you have time to put down your thoughts without interruptions.

## What You Do

1. Begin each entry in your diary with the day and date. This step helps you remember when things happened. You can go back and read about what you did a week ago, a month ago, or a year ago.
2. Write about anything that interests you. Write about what you did today. Describe whom you saw, what you studied, and songs you heard.
3. Write about your feelings. Describe what makes you happy or sad. Give your opinions about things you see, hear, or read.
4. Write in your diary regularly.

*Sarah attended or taught school almost all of her life. She is pictured here at her graduation from Upper Iowa University in 1920.*

Sarah Gillespie Huftalen.
A.B. aug. 26. 1920 U.I.U.
Rank A + A+ B+ B+

# Afterword

At age 17, Sarah began a teaching career that would last 54 years. Her first teaching job was at a one-room school not far from Manchester. In September 1892, Sarah married William H. Huftalen. Sarah continued teaching in different schools throughout the area until 1935.

Sarah moved back to the family farm and spent most of her time collecting and organizing family letters, photographs, and diaries. She sent these materials to the State Historical Society of Iowa in February of 1952. Sarah died two years later, on February 11, 1955, shortly after selling the family farm to one of her former students.

*Before Sarah died, she collected family letters, photographs, and diaries. She sent this material to the State Historical Society of Iowa so that people could learn what it was like to be a pioneer farm girl.*

# *Timeline*

The Northern states and the Southern states fight the Civil War (1861–1865).

The 19th amendment to the constitution gives women the right to vote.

| 1864 | 1877 | 1881 | 1892 | 1919 |
|------|------|------|------|------|

Sarah Gillespie is born.

Sarah begins her diary.

Sarah begins her career as a teacher.

Sarah marries William (Billie) Henry Huftalen

Japanese forces
bomb Pearl Harbor
in the Hawaiian
Islands. The United
States enters World
War II (1939–1945).

The U.S. Supreme
Court orders the end
of school segregation.

**1935**  **1941**  **1952**  **1955**

Sarah retires
from
teaching.

Sarah donates her
diary to the State
Historical Society
of Iowa.

Sarah dies on
February 11.

# *Words to Know*

**agriculture** (AG-ruh-kul-chur)—the practice of growing crops and raising livestock for food

**barter** (BAR-tur)—to trade by exchanging food or other goods rather than using money

**chambree or chambray** (SHAM-bray)—a lightweight clothing fabric

**cholera** (KOL-ur-uh)—a disease that causes severe sickness and diarrhea

**collateral** (KAH-laht-ah-rel)—offering something of value as security for repaying a loan

**delicacy** (DEL-uh-kuh-see)—a delicious food or drink

**foolscap** ( FOOLZ-kap)—writing paper

**gosling** (GOZZ-ling)—a baby goose

**perforate** (PUR-fuh-rayt)—to make a row of small holes through paper or other material

**prediction** (pre-DIK-shuhn)—telling what will happen in the future

**premium** (PREE-mee-uhm)—a prize

**rod** (ROD)—a unit of length about equal to 5 ½ yards [5 meters]

**Sabbath** (SAB-uhth)—the day of rest and worship in some religions

**slough** (SLEW)— a ditch filled with deep mud

**smother** (SMUTH-ur)—to cover someone's nose and mouth so that the person cannot breathe

**spunky** (SPUNK-ee)—full of spirit

**straw-work** (STRAW-wurk)—decorative items made from straw

**whip-stalk** (WIP-stawk)—the handle of a whip

# Internet Sites

**America's West—Development
and History**
http://www.americanwest.com

**The Gibbs Farm Musuem,
St. Paul, Minnesota**
http://www.rchs.com/gbbsfm2.htm

**Living History Farms**
http://www.ioweb.com/lhf

**Pioneers**
http://tqjunior.advanced.org/6400

# To Learn More

**Gunderson, Mary**. *Pioneer Farm Cooking*. Exploring History through Simple Recipes.
Mankato, Minn.: Blue Earth Books, 2000.

**Hester, Sallie**. *A Covered-Wagon Girl: The Diary of Sallie Hester. 1849-1850*. Edited by
Christy Steele with Ann Hodgson. Diaries, Letters, and Memoirs. Mankato, Minn.: Blue
Earth Books, 2000.

**Huftalen**, **Sarah Gillespie**. *All Will Yet Be Well: The Diary of Sarah Gillespie Huftalen,
1873-1952*. Edited by Suzanne L. Bunkers. Iowa City, Iowa: Iowa City Press, 1993.

*My Prairie Year: Based on the Diary of Elenore Plaisted*. Adapted by Brett Harvey.
New York: Holiday House, 1996.

# Places to Write and Visit

Agriculture Museum
P.O. Box 9724, Station T
Ottawa, ON  K1G 5A3
Canada

Living History Farms
2600 NW 11th Street
Urbandale, IA 50322

Oliver Kelley Farm
15788 Kelley Farm Road
Elk River, MN 44330

Pioneer Farm Museum
7716 Ohop Valley Road
Eatonvile, WA 98328

# INDEX